THE ILLINOIS LOBBYIST SURVEY

PRINCIPAL INVESTIGATORS

RONALD D. HEDLUND
SAMUEL C. PATTERSON

LABORATORY FOR POLITICAL RESEARCH
STATE UNIVERSITY OF IOWA

MARCH - APRIL, 1963

ICPR EDITION
FIRST PRINTING, 1969
SECOND PRINTING, 1975

INTER-UNIVERSITY CONSORTIUM FOR POLITICAL RESEARCH
BOX 1248
ANN ARBOR, MICHIGAN 48106

ISBN 0-89138-006-X
LIBRARY OF CONGRESS CATALOG CARD NUMBER 75-38490

ACKNOWLEDGMENT OF ASSISTANCE

ALL MANUSCRIPTS UTILIZING DATA MADE AVAILABLE THROUGH THE CONSORTIUM SHOULD ACKNOWLEDGE THAT FACT AS WELL AS IDENTIFY THE ORIGINAL COLLECTOR OF THE DATA. THE ICPR COUNCIL URGES ALL USERS OF ICPR DATA FACILITIES TO FOLLOW SOME ADAPTATION OF THIS STATEMENT WITH THE PARENTHESES INDICATING ITEMS TO BE FILLED IN APPROPRIATELY OR DELETED BY THE INDIVIDUAL USER.

THE DATA (AND TABULATIONS) UTILIZED IN THIS (PUBLICATION) WERE MADE AVAILABLE (IN PART) BY THE INTER-UNIVERSITY CONSORTIUM FOR POLITICAL RESEARCH. THE DATA WERE ORIGINALLY COLLECTED BY RONALD D. HEDLUND AND SAMUEL C. PATTERSON. NEITHER THE ORIGINAL COLLECTOR OF THE DATA NOR THE CONSORTIUM BEAR ANY RESPONSIBILITY FOR THE ANALYSES OR INTERPRETATIONS PRESENTED HERE.

IN ORDER TO PROVIDE FUNDING AGENCIES WITH ESSENTIAL INFORMATION ABOUT THE USE OF ARCHIVAL RESOURCES, AND TO FACILITATE THE EXCHANGE OF INFORMATION ABOUT ICPR PARTICIPANTS' RESEARCH ACTIVITIES, EACH USER OF THE ICPR DATA FACILITIES IS EXPECTED TO SEND TWO COPIES OF EACH COMPLETED MANUSCRIPT (OR THESIS ABSTRACT) TO THE CONSORTIUM. PLEASE INDICATE IN THE COVER LETTER WHICH DATA WERE USED.

Study Description and Sampling Information

The Illinois Lobbyist Survey by Ronald Hedlund and Samuel Patterson was designed to provide an empirical base for what the authors believed to be rather broad generalizations about lobbyists and the lobbying process.
The data were collected from questionnaires mailed during 1964 to 398 individuals registered as lobbyists in Illinois. The first mailing took place in March of 1964 and was followed by two additional mailings separated by intervals of approximately three weeks. In addition to standard demographic information, the study contains variables dealing with the following general categories: previous political experience, perceptions of the Illinois legislature and Illinois legislators, perceptions of the lobbyist's role, judgments on specific aspects of a lobbyist's behavior, and finally, measures of the lobbyist's political philosophy.
Summarized in the table below is a breakdown of the sample by organization, with the response rate for each type of organization displayed on the right.

Type of organization the lobbyist represents	Percent of the total sample (N=229)	Response rate (Percent)
Professional	14	73
Educational	7	73
Financial	11	60
Corporation	8	44
Trade and Industrial	23	50
Agricultural	3	78
Labor Unions	10	51
Governmental Units	11	62
Civic	7	63
Religious and Charitable	3	60
Veterans	1	100
All others	1	33

The results of this investigation are discussed by Ronald D. Hedlund and Samuel C. Patterson in "Personal Attributes, Political Orientations, and Occupational Perspectives of Lobbyists: The Case of Illinois," Iowa Business Digest, Vol. 37, No. 11, (1966), pp. 3-11.
....

Processing Information

This study was processed according to the ICPR's standard processing procedures for intermediate data sets. The code categories were recoded to eliminate amps, dashes, blanks, or any other alphabetic punch. Where a code category was recoded, the original value has been retained in the codebook between asterisks at the end of the code text. No attempt was made to recode variables to conform to standard

ICPR coding conventions. Illegal (wild) codes (i.e., codes not present in the investigator's legitimate list of codes) were noted but not corrected. In addition, no attempt was made to do any consistency checking and as a result the frequencies for some variables do not tabulate as they would if consistency had been forced between variables.

Certain other features of this codebook deserve attention. Each variable is headed by a variable name which, in most cases, contains several abbreviated words. If necessary, these abbreviations can be translated by referring to the unabbreviated variable name appearing in the table of contents below. Those variable names preceded by an "X" indicate a variable dependent on some other variable due to the structure of the questionnaire. Each variable is also given a "variable number" and "reference number" which, in this codebook, are identical. The difference between the two is not material except in the case of future custom codebooks.

Certain codes are labeled as missing data codes ("MD"). This information is used by some ISR analysis programs. It is the only meaning or use of this specification. It does not mean that the user should not or cannot use the codes in a substantive role. "GE," used in the specification of missing data means "greater than or equal to."

Please note that for many users the only relevant information in the variable header is the deck and column number, which are found on the third line on the right.

Frequencies for multiple response variables are cumulative.

Information set in "greater than" and "less than" signs (<>) will be found in the codebook. For example: <For the full question text of this variable see Ref. No. 21>. In all cases this represents information added by the processor in the course of preparing the codebook.

The present edition of this study was done by John R. Petrocik.

CONTENTS

VARIABLE NUMBER	VARIABLE NAME	PAGE NO.
1	STUDY IDENTIFICATION	1
2	INTERVIEW NUMBER	

RESIDENCE, WHERE BORN, AGE, SEX

3	PLACE OF RESIDENCE -- LOCATION	
4	PLACE OF RESIDENCE -- SIZE	
5	PLACE OF BIRTH -- LOCATION	2
6	PLACE OF BIRTH -- SIZE	
7	STATE OF BIRTH	3
8	SEX	5
9	AGE	
10	CITY WHERE R WAS REARED -- SIZE	

R'S PRESENT AND PAST OCCUPATIONS; FATHER'S OCCUPATION

11	PRIMARY OCCUPATION OF R	6
12	OTHER TYPES OF WORK R HAS DONE	7
13	R EMPLOYED BY WHOM	9
14	TITLE OF R'S PRESENT POSITION	
15	EMPLOYMENT PREVIOUSLY HELD BY R	10
16	OCCUPATION OF R'S FATHER	11

RELIGION AND EDUCATION

17	RELIGION	13
18	HIGHEST LEVEL OF FORMAL EDUCATION	
19	XR'S COLLEGE MAJOR	14

PUBLIC OFFICES HELD BY R, LENGTH OF TENURE

20	GOVERNMENTAL POSITIONS HELD BY R	
21	XTYPE OF LOCAL POSITION R HELD	15
22	XTENURE IN LOCAL POSITION	
23	XTYPE OF COUNTY POSITION R HELD	16
24	XTENURE IN COUNTY POSITION	
25	XTYPE OF STATE LEGISLATIVE POSITION R HELD	17
26	XTENURE IN STATE LEGISLATIVE POSITION	
27	XTYPE OF STATE EXECUTIVE POSITION R HELD	
28	XTENURE IN STATE EXECUTIVE POSITION	18
29	XTYPE OF FEDERAL EXECUTIVE POSITION R HELD	
30	XTENURE IN FEDERAL EXECUTIVE POSITION	19
31	XTYPE OF CONGRESSIONAL POSITION R HELD	
32	XTENURE IN THE CONGRESS	20
33	HAS ANY MEMBER OF R'S FAMILY HELD OFFICE	

CONTENTS

VARIABLE NUMBER	VARIABLE NAME	PAGE NO.
	POLITICAL PARTIES; AFFILIATION AND OFFICES HELD	
34	R'S PARTY AFFILIATION	20
35	HAS R HELD PARTY OFFICE	21
36	HAS R CONTRIBUTED TO A POLITICAL PARTY	
	INCOME, INCOME FROM LOBBYING	
37	R'S TOTAL INCOME	
38	PERCENT OF ALL INCOME FROM LOBBYING	22
	GROUPS REPRESENTED, TENURE AS LOBBYIST	
39	R LOBBYIST FOR HOW LONG	
40	NUMBER OF GROUPS R REPRESENTED IN 1963	23
41	TYPES OF GROUPS R REPRESENTS	
42	HAS R ALWAYS REPRESENTED SAME GROUP(S)	24
43	XOTHER GROUPS R REPRESENTED	
44	WILL R REMAIN A LOBBYIST	
	TIME SPENT LOBBYING	
45	TIME R SPENDS LOBBYING DURING SESSIONS	25
46	TIME R SPENDS LOBBYING BETWEEN SESSIONS	
	WHY R IS A LOBBYIST	
47	FIRST REASON R IS A LOBBYIST	26
48	SECOND REASON R IS A LOBBYIST	
49	THIRD REASON R IS A LOBBYIST	27
	ASPECTS OF WORK R LIKES, DISLIKES	
50	ASPECT OF WORK R LIKES MOST	28
51	ASPECT OF WORK R LIKES SECOND MOST	
52	ASPECT OF WORK R LIKES THIRD MOST	29
53	ASPECT OF WORK R LIKES LEAST	
54	ASPECT OF WORK R LIKES SECOND LEAST	30
55	ASPECT OF WORK R LIKES THIRD LEAST	31
	QUALITIES NEEDED BY A LOBBYIST	
56	LOBBYIST'S MOST NEEDED QUALITY	
57	LOBBYIST'S SECOND MOST NEEDED QUALITY	32
58	LOBBYIST'S THIRD MOST NEEDED QUALITY	

CONTENTS

VARIABLE NUMBER	VARIABLE NAME	PAGE NO.
	LOBBYIST'S MAJOR ACTIVITIES	
59	LOBBYIST'S MAJOR ACTIVITY	33
60	LOBBYIST'S SECOND MAJOR ACTIVITY	34
61	LOBBYIST'S THIRD MAJOR ACTIVITY	
	LOBBYING ACTIVITIES EXPECTED OF R	
62	ACTIVITY MOST EXPECTED OF R	35
63	ACTIVITY EXPECTED OF R SECOND	
64	ACTIVITY EXPECTED OF R THIRD	36
	LOBBYING ACTIVITIES R FINDS MOST DIFFICULT	
65	ACTIVITY R FINDS MOST DIFFICULT AS LOBBYIST	37
66	ACTIVITY R FINDS SECOND MOST DIFFICULT	
67	ACTIVITY R FINDS THIRD MOST DIFFICULT	38
	LOBBYING ACTIVITIES AT WHICH R IS MOST SUCCESSFUL	
68	ACTIVITY AT WHICH R HAS MOST SUCCESS	
69	ACTIVITY AT WHICH R HAS SECOND MOST SUCCESS	39
70	ACTIVITY AT WHICH R HAS THIRD MOST SUCCESS	
	NUMBER OF LEGISLATORS R TALKS TO	
71	NUMBER OF LEGISLATORS R TALKS WITH PER SESSION	40
	LEGISLATION R'S GROUP IS INTERESTED IN	
72	LEGISLATION R'S GROUP MOST INTERESTED IN	41
73	LEGISLATION R'S GROUP SECOND MOST INTERESTED IN	
74	LEGISLATION R'S GROUP THIRD MOST INTERESTED IN	42
	LEGISLATORS REPRESENT WHOM	
75	WHOM DOES R THINK LEGISLATORS SHOULD REPRESENT	
76	WHOM DOES R THINK LEGISLATORS DO REPRESENT	43
	WHERE R CONCENTRATES LOBBYING	
77	STAGE OF THE LEGISLATIVE PROCESS AT WHICH R CONCENTRATES HIS ACTIVITY MOST	
78	STAGE OF THE LEGISLATIVE PROCESS AT WHICH R CONCENTRATES HIS ACTIVITY SECOND MOST	44
79	STAGE OF THE LEGISLATIVE PROCESS AT WHICH R CONCENTRATES HIS ACTIVITY THIRD MOST	

CONTENTS

VARIABLE NUMBER	VARIABLE NAME	PAGE NO.
	EFFECTIVENESS OF DIFFERENT LOBBYING TECHNIQUES	
80	FREQUENCY OF R'S WORK WITH BOTH PARTIES	45
81	R'S VIEW OF THE EFFECTIVENESS OF PRESENTING PERSONAL VIEWPOINT	
82	R'S VIEW OF THE EFFECTIVENESS OF PRESENTING RESEARCH	46
83	R'S VIEW OF THE EFFECTIVENESS OF PRESENTING COMMITTEE TESTIMONY	
84	R'S VIEW OF THE EFFECTIVENESS OF PRESENTING CONTACT	47
85	R'S VIEW OF THE EFFECTIVENESS OF PRESENTING FRIENDS	
86	R'S VIEW OF THE EFFECTIVENESS OF PRESENTING TELEGRAM CAMPAIGNS	48
87	R'S VIEW OF THE EFFECTIVENESS OF PRESENTING RELATIONS CAMPAIGN	
88	R'S VIEW OF THE EFFECTIVENESS OF PRESENTING A LEGISLATOR'S VOTING RECORD	49
89	R'S VIEW OF THE EFFECTIVENESS OF PRESENTING ENTERTAINMENT FOR LEGISLATORS	
90	R'S VIEW OF THE EFFECTIVENESS OF PRESENTING CONTRIBUTIONS	50
91	R'S VIEW OF THE EFFECTIVENESS OF PRESENTING WORK	
	IMPORTANCE AND FREQUENCY OF R'S WORK WITH OTHER LOBBYISTS	
92	IMPORTANCE OF WORKING WITH OTHER LOBBYING GROUPS	
93	FREQUENCY OF R'S JOINT EFFORT WITH LOBBYISTS FOR PROFESSIONAL GROUPS	51
94	FREQUENCY OF R'S JOINT EFFORT WITH LOBBYISTS FOR EDUCATIONAL GROUPS	52
95	FREQUENCY OF R'S JOINT EFFORT WITH LOBBYISTS FOR FARM GROUPS	
96	FREQUENCY OF R'S JOINT EFFORT WITH LOBBYISTS FOR FINANCIAL GROUPS	53
97	FREQUENCY OF R'S JOINT EFFORT WITH LOBBYISTS FOR LABOR UNIONS	
98	FREQUENCY OF R'S JOINT EFFORT WITH LOBBYISTS FOR GOVERNMENTAL UNITS	54
99	FREQUENCY OF R'S JOINT EFFORT WITH LOBBYISTS FOR CIVIC GROUPS	
100	FREQUENCY OF R'S JOINT EFFORT WITH LOBBYISTS FOR CORPORATIONS	55

CONTENTS

VARIABLE NUMBER	VARIABLE NAME	PAGE NO.
101	FREQUENCY OF R'S JOINT EFFORT WITH LOBBYISTS FOR RELIGIOUS AND CHARITABLE GROUPS	
102	FREQUENCY OF R'S JOINT EFFORT WITH LOBBYISTS FOR VETERAN'S GROUPS	56
103	FREQUENCY OF R'S JOINT EFFORT WITH LOBBYISTS FOR TRADE AND INDUSTRIAL GROUPS	

MOST SUCCESSFUL LOBBYING GROUPS

104	MOST SUCCESSFUL LOBBYING GROUP	57
105	SECOND MOST SUCCESSFUL LOBBYING GROUP	58
106	THIRD MOST SUCCESSFUL LOBBYING GROUP	

LIBERAL-CONSERVATIVE INDICATORS

107	FEDERAL GOVERNMENT'S ROLE IN ENDING DISCRIMINATION	59
108	STATE ADMINISTRATION OF SOCIAL SECURITY	
109	U.S. RECOGNITION OF RED CHINA	60
110	R'S JUDGMENT OF ADC PROGRAMS	
111	FOREIGN AID FOR AMERICAN ALLIES ONLY	

POLITICAL PHILOSOPHY AND ROLE PERCEPTION OF R

112	LIBERAL-CONSERVATIVE INDEX	61
113	R'S PERCEPTION OF A LOBBYIST'S ROLE	

THE ILLINOIS LOBBYIST SURVEY   PAGE   1

VAR 0001   REF 0001   DATA SET ID-'7283'
   NAME-STUDY NUMBER   NO MISSING DATA CODES
      LOC   1 WIDTH 4   DK 1 COL 1- 4

              Study Identification (7283)
              ....

                   '01'   DK 1 COL 5- 6
                   ....

VAR 0002   REF 0002   DATA SET ID-'7283'
   NAME-INTERVIEW NUMBER   NO MISSING DATA CODES
      LOC   5 WIDTH 3   DK 1 COL 7- 9

              Interview Number
              ....

VAR 0003   REF 0003   DATA SET ID-'7283'
   NAME-PLACE OF RES-ADDRESS   NO MISSING DATA CODES
      LOC   8 WIDTH 1   DK 1 COL 10

              Place of Residence (by location; if not ascertainable,
              then mailing address used).
              ....

         69   1. Chicago
         39   2. Suburban Chicago (also DuPage and Lake counties)
         57   3. Springfield
          5   4. Quad-city area (Rock Island, Moline,
                      East Moline, Milan)
          3   5. Rockford
          2   6. Decator
          5   7. Peoria
         47   8. Other (in Illinois)   *-*
          2   9. Out of State *&*

VAR 0004   REF 0004   DATA SET ID-'7283'
   NAME-PLACE OF RES-SIZE   MD=GE 9
      LOC   9 WIDTH 1   DK 1 COL 11

              Place of Residence (by size)
              ....

THE ILLINOIS LOBBYIST SURVEY

(CONTINUED)

129	1. Large city (over 50,000)
45	2. Medium size city (10,000-50,000)
16	3. Small size city (2,500-10,000)
5	4. City under 2,500
6	5. Farm
28	9. NA

VAR 0005   REF 0005   DATA SET ID-'7283'
NAME-PLACE OF BIRTH-ADRS   MD=GE 91
    LOC   10   WIDTH   2   DK   1 COL 12-13

A1. Where were you born. (City and State)

54	01. Chicago
7	02. Suburban Chicago
7	03. Springfield
3	04. Quad-city area
2	05. Rockford
1	06. Decator
2	07. East St. Louis
1	08. Peoria
64	09. Other city "downstate" *&*
86	91. INAP., (not born in Illinois) *0*
2	99. NA *9*

VAR 0006   REF 0006   DATA SET ID-'7283'
NAME-PLACE OF BIRTH-SIZE   MD=GE 9
    LOC   12   WIDTH   1   DK   1 COL 14

Place of birth. (Size of city)

93	1. Large city (over 50,000)
37	2. Medium size city (10,000-50,000)
28	3. Small size city (2,500-10,000)
45	4. City under 2,500
17	5. Farm
9	9. NA

THE ILLINOIS LOBBYIST SURVEY   PAGE   3

VAR 0007   REF 0007   DATA SET ID-'7283'
   NAME-STATE OF BIRTH   MD=GE 99
      LOC   13 WIDTH 2   DK 1 COL 15-16

             State of birth.   (First digit indicates region.)
             ....

             New England

         1   01. Connecticut
         0   02. Maine
         3   03. Massachusetts
         0   04. New Hampshire
         1   05. Rhode Island
         0   06. Vermont

             Middle Atlantic

         1   11. Delaware
         0   12. New Jersey
         6   13. New York
         3   14. Pennsylvania

             East North Central

       141   21. Illinois
         6   22. Indiana
         1   23. Michigan
         6   24. Ohio
         5   25. Wisconsin

             West North Central

         6   31. Iowa
         2   32. Kansas
         2   33. Minnesota
         4   34. Missouri
         1   35. Nebraska
         2   36. North Dakota
         3   37. South Dakota

THE ILLINOIS LOBBYIST SURVEY

(CONTINUED)

Solid South

2	41.	Alabama
2	42.	Arkansas
0	43.	Florida
1	44.	Georgia
0	45.	Louisiana
0	46.	Mississippi
2	47.	North Carolina
0	48.	South Carolina
0	49.	Texas
2	40.	Virginia

Border States

6	51.	Kentucky
0	52.	Maryland
2	53.	Oklahoma
2	54.	Tennessee
0	55.	Washington, D.C.
0	56.	West Virginia

Mountain States

0	61.	Arizona
4	62.	Colorado
0	63.	Idaho
2	64.	Montana
0	65.	Nevada
0	66.	New Mexico
0	67.	Utah
1	68.	Wyoming

Western States

0	71.	California
0	72.	Oregon
0	73.	Washington
1	79.	NA (Response was "a western state") *70*
6	88.	Foreign Country
2	99.	NA

THE ILLINOIS LOBBYIST SURVEY   PAGE   5

VAR 0008   REF 0008   DATA SET ID-'7283'
    NAME-SEX   NO MISSING DATA CODES
       LOC   15 WIDTH   1   DK 1 COL 17

             Sex
             ...

       217   1. Male
        12   2. Female

VAR 0009   REF 0009   DATA SET ID-'7283'
    NAME-AGE   MD=GE 9
       LOC   16 WIDTH   1   DK 1 COL 18

             A2. What is your age (years).
             ....

         3   1. Under 30
        17   2. 31-35
        30   3. 36-40
        31   4. 41-45
        31   5. 46-50
        35   6. 51-55
        31   7. 56-60
        22   8. 61-65
        26   0. Over 65

         3   9. NA

VAR 0010   REF 0010   DATA SET ID-'7283'
    NAME-CITY WHERE R REARED-SIZE   MD=GE 9
       LOC   17 WIDTH   1   DK 1 COL 19

             A3. When you were growing up did you live mainly:
             ....

             SEE NOTE(S) 1

       101   1. In a large city (over 50,000)
        38   2. In a medium size city (10,000-50,000)
        55   3. In a small city (under 10,000)
        35   4. On a farm

THE ILLINOIS LOBBYIST SURVEY

(CONTINUED)
....

    0   9. NA

VAR 0011   REF 0011   DATA SET ID-'7283'
NAME-OCCUPATION OF RESPONDENT   MD=GE 99
   LOC   18 WIDTH 2   DK 1 COL 20-21

A4. What do you consider your main occupation.

```
  5      00. Retired
 12      01. Lobbyist
  8      02. Legislative research
 16      03. Public relations
 48      04. Association executive
  5      05. Elected official (government)
  1      06. Appointed official (government)
 14      07. Labor executive
  5      08. Civil Servant -- police, etc.
```

Professional and Technical

```
  1      10. Accountants and auditors
  0      11. Clergymen
  2      12. Public school teachers
  0      13. Dentists
  3      14. Engineers
 42      15. Lawyers and judges (not employed by a corporation)
  0      16. Physicians and surgeons
  0      17. Social and welfare workers
  6      18. Other professional and technical
  8      19. Trained nurse, student nurse, practical nurse
```

Self-employed Businessmen; Managers and Officials

```
  4      21. Self-employed commercial businessman
 15      22. Lawyer with a corporation or association
 14      25. Managers, officials, and proprietors
```

Clerical and Sales

  0   31. Bookkeeper

THE ILLINOIS LOBBYIST SURVEY   PAGE   7

             (CONTINUED)
             ....

        0   32. Stenographers, typists, and secretaries
        2   33. Store operator
        1   35. Other clerical
        0   36. Sales: Higher status traveling or outside goods
        1   37. Sales: Higher status outside services
        5   38. Sales: Inside sales, real estate broker

             Skilled Workers

        0   41. Self-employed skilled craftsman
        0   42. Foreman
        2   43. Other skilled craftsman
        3   44. Semi-skilled operative and kindred workers

             Unskilled Laborers

        2   51. Farmers
        0   52. Unskilled laborers

             Other

        1   60. The Arts -- Writing, etc.
        1   61. Journalism
        1   62. Mother and housewife

        1   99. NA

VAR 0012   REF 0012   DATA SET ID-'7283'
   NAME-OTHER TYPES OF EMPLT   MD=GE 88
      LOC   20 WIDTH 2   DK 1 COL 22-23

             What other kinds of employment do you have.
             ....

        1   00. Retired
        7   01. Lobbyist
        0   02. Legislative research
        0   03. Public relations
        6   04. Association executive
        1   05. Elected official (government)
        2   06. Appointed official (government)

THE ILLINOIS LOBBYIST SURVEY

(CONTINUED)
----

2   07. Labor executive
0   08. Civil Servant -- police, etc.

Professional and Technical

1   10. Accountants and auditors
0   11. Clergymen
1   12. Public school teachers
0   13. Dentists
0   14. Engineers
2   15. Lawyers and judges (not employed by a corporation)
0   16. Physicians and surgeons
0   17. Social and welfare workers
1   18. Other professional and technical
0   19. Trained nurse, student nurse, practical nurse

Self-employed Businessmen; Managers and Officials

0   21. Self-employed commercial businessman
1   22. Lawyer with a corporation or association
5   25. Managers, officials, and proprietors

Clerical and Sales

0   31. Bookkeeper
1   32. Stenographers, typists, and secretaries
0   33. Store operator
0   35. Other clerical
0   36. Sales: Higher status traveling or outside goods
0   37. Sales: Higher status outside services
2   38. Sales: Inside sales, real estate broker

Skilled Workers

0   41. Self-employed skilled craftsmen
0   42. Foreman
0   43. Other skilled craftsmen
1   44. Semi-skilled operative and kindred workers

Unskilled Laborers

THE ILLINOIS LOBBYIST SURVEY

(CONTINUED)

```
    0      51.  Farmers
    0      52.  Unskilled laborers
```

Other

```
    0      60.  The Arts -- writing, etc.
    0      61.  Journalism
    1      62.  Mother and housewife

    1      88.  ILLEGAL CODE

  193      96.  R has no other occupation  *Blank*
```

VAR 0013   REF 0013   DATA SET ID-'7283'
NAME-BY WHOM EMPLOYED   MD=GE 7
    LOC   22 WIDTH 1   DK   1 COL 24

By whom are you employed.

```
  135     1.  Group R represents
   59     2.  Self
   12     3.  Governmental unit

   23     7.  Other  *&*
```

VAR 0014   REF 0014   DATA SET ID-'7283'
NAME-XTITLE OF PSNT POSITION   MD=0 OR GE 9
    LOC   23 WIDTH 1   DK   1 COL 25

A5. What is the specific title or name of your present
position.

```
   26     1.  Lobbyist and related positions
   39     2.  Partner in law firm
    9     3.  Partner in public relations firm (or owner of)
   74     4.  Association executive
    4     5.  Owner or partner in another type of company
    5     6.  Government employee  *8*
   33     7.  Managerial  *-*
```

THE ILLINOIS LOBBYIST SURVEY

PAGE 10

(CONTINUED)
....

```
  2      8.  Laborer  *0*
 10      9.  NA
 27      0.  INAP., <no further explanation in the investigator's
             codebook>  *&*
```

```
VAR 0015                          REF 0015              DATA SET ID-'7283'
    NAME-EMPLT PRVSLY HAD BY R      MD=GE 96             MULT RESPS    4
    LOC   24  WIDTH  2              DK  1 COL 26-33
```

A6. What are some other jobs you have previously held.
....

```
  0    00.  Retired
  4    01.  Lobbyist
  5    02.  Legislative research
 10    03.  Public relations
  6    04.  Association executive
 11    05.  Elected official (government)
 14    06.  Appointed official (government)
  4    07.  Labor executive
 14    08.  Civil Servant -- police, etc.
```

Professional and Technical

```
  6    10.  Accountants and auditors
  0    11.  Clergymen
 24    12.  Public school teachers
  0    13.  Dentists
  5    14.  Engineers
  4    15.  Lawyers and judges (not employed by a corporation)
  0    16.  Physicians and surgeons
  0    17.  Social and welfare workers
 12    18.  Other professional and technical
  3    19.  Trained nurse, student nurse, practical nurse
```

Self-employed Businessmen; Managers and Officials

```
 12    21.  Self-employed commercial businessman
  5    22.  Lawyer with a corporation or association
 24    25.  Managers, officials, and proprietors
```

THE ILLINOIS LOBBYIST SURVEY   PAGE 11

(CONTINUED)
. . . .

        Clerical and Sales

1	31.	Bookkeeper
0	32.	Stenographers, typists, and secretaries
3	33.	Store operator
8	35.	Other clerical
8	36.	Sales: Higher status traveling or outside goods
3	37.	Sales: Higher status outside services
5	38.	Sales: Inside sales, real estate broker

        Skilled Workers

0	41.	Self-employed skilled craftsman
1	42.	Foreman
8	43.	Other skilled craftsmen
15	44.	Semi-skilled operative and kindred workers

        Unskilled Laborers

3	51.	Farmers
14	52.	Unskilled laborers

        Other

4	60.	The Arts -- writing, etc.
15	61.	Journalism
0	62.	Mother and housewife
665	96.	R has held only one position or offered no further response *Blank*

VAR 0016   REF 0016   DATA SET ID-'7283'
  NAME-OCC OF FATHER   MD=GE 90
    LOC 32 WIDTH 2   DK 1 COL 34-35

    A7. What was your father's principal occupation during most of his life.
. . . .

0	00.	Retired
0	01.	Lobbyist

THE ILLINOIS LOBBYIST SURVEY

(CONTINUED)

0	02.	Legislative research
1	03.	Public relations
0	04.	Association executive
1	05.	Elected official (government)
2	06.	Appointed official (government)
1	07.	Labor executive
3	08.	Civil Servant -- police, etc.

Professional and Technical

3	10.	Accountants and auditors
3	11.	Clergymen
5	12.	Public school teachers
0	13.	Dentists
2	14.	Engineers
16	15.	Lawyers and judges (not employed by a corporation)
2	16.	Physicians and surgeons
1	17.	Social and welfare workers
9	18.	Other professional and technical
0	19.	Trained nurse, student nurse, practical nurse

Self-employed Businessmen; Managers and Officials

17	21.	Self-employed commercial businessman
1	22.	Lawyer with a corporation or association
12	25.	Managers, officials, and proprietors

Clerical and Sales

0	31.	Bookkeeper
0	32.	Stenographers, typists, and secretaries
14	33.	Store operator
4	35.	Other clerical
7	36.	Sales: Higher status traveling or outside goods
0	37.	Sales: Higher status outside services
16	38.	Sales: Inside sales, real estate broker

Skilled Workers

3	41.	Self-employed skilled craftsman
2	42.	Foreman
14	43.	Other skilled craftsmen
26	44.	Semi-skilled operatives and kindred workers

THE ILLINOIS LOBBYIST SURVEY   PAGE 13

               (CONTINUED)

               Unskilled Laborers
         37   51. Farmers
         16   52. Unskilled laborers

               Other
         1   60. The Arts -- writing, etc.
         1   61. Journalism
         0   62. Mother and housewife

         1   90. Other   *Blank*
         8   99. NA

VAR 0017   REF 0017   DATA SET ID-'7283'
   NAME-RELIGION   MD=GE 7
      LOC 34 WIDTH 1   DK 1 COL 36

               A8. What is your religious preference.
               ....

               SEE NOTE(S) 1

         3   0. None *5*

         72   1. Catholic
         139   2. Protestant
         5   3. Jewish

         5   7. Other *4*
         5   9. NA

VAR 0018   REF 0018   DATA SET ID-'7283'
   NAME-HIGHEST ED LEVEL   NO MISSING DATA CODES
      LOC 35 WIDTH 1   DK 1 COL 37

               A9. What is your highest level of formal educational
               training.
               ....

THE ILLINOIS LOBBYIST SURVEY   PAGE 14

    (CONTINUED)

    SEE NOTE(S) 1

    3   1. Elementary
   11   2. Some high school
   22   3. Completed high school
   45   4. Some college
   39   5. Completed college
   20   6. Some graduate work
   23   7. Masters degree
    1   8. Ph.D. degree
   65   0. Law degree

VAR 0019   REF 0019   DATA SET ID-'7283'
  NAME-XCOLLEGE MAJOR   MD=GE 90
    LOC   36 WIDTH 2   DK 1 COL 38-39

    A9. If you have attended college what was your major.

   37   01. Business and associated fields, accounting, economics
   16   02. Pre-law
   25   03. Political Science
    4   04. Psychology
    7   05. Journalism
   11   06. Engineering
    7   07. English
   11   08. Science
    9   09. Education *0*

   29   90. Other *&*
   36   91. INAP., coded 1-3 in REF. NO. 18 or no college work *-*
   37   99. NA *9*

VAR 0020   REF 0020   DATA SET ID-'7283'
  NAME-HELD GOVT POSITION   MD=GE 9
    LOC   38 WIDTH 1   DK 1 COL 40

    A10. Have you ever held any elected or appointed governmental positions.

THE ILLINOIS LOBBYIST SURVEY

(CONTINUED)

```
    105       1. Yes
    124       5. No

      0       9. NA
```

```
VAR 0021                      REF 0021              DATA SET ID-'7283'
    NAME-XTYPE LCL POS HELD       MD=0
        LOC   39 WIDTH  1         DK  1 COL 41
```

A10a. If YES,<to REF. NO. 20> in what units of government have you served, what were the types of positions held, and what was the approximate length of time you held each position. (Check where applicable)

Type of position -- Local

SEE NOTE(S) 1

```
     20       1. Elected
     30       2. Appointed
      2       3. Both

    177       0. INAP., coded 5 or 9 in REF. NO. 20, or held no
                 position at this level  *Blank*
```

```
VAR 0022                      REF 0022              DATA SET ID-'7283'
    NAME-XTENURE LCL POS          MD=0 OR GE 9
        LOC   40 WIDTH  1         DK  1 COL 42
```

Length of tenure -- Local.

<For the full question text of this variable see Ref. No. 21>

SEE NOTE(S) 1

```
     25       1. 0-5 years
      9       2. 5-10 years
     13       3. More than 10 years
```

THE ILLINOIS LOBBYIST SURVEY

(CONTINUED)
....

```
         5         9.  NA
       177         0.  INAP., coded 5 or 9 in REF. NO. 20, or held no
                       position at this level  *Blank*
```

VAR 0023   REF 0023   DATA SET ID-'7283'
   NAME-XTYPE CNTY POS HELD   MD=0 OR GE 9
      LOC   41 WIDTH 1   DK 1 COL 43

Type of position -- County.
....

<For the full question text of this variable see Ref. No. 21>

SEE NOTE(S) 1

```
        15         1.  Elected
        20         2.  Appointed
         2         3.  Both

         1         9.  NA
       191         0.  INAP., coded 5 or 9 in REF. NO. 20, or held no
                       position at this level  *Blank*
```

VAR 0024   REF 0024   DATA SET ID-'7283'
   NAME-XTENURE CNTY POS   MD=0 OR GE 9
      LOC   42 WIDTH 1   DK 1 COL 44

Length of tenure -- County.
....

<For the full question text of this variable see Ref. No. 21>

SEE NOTE(S) 1

```
        15         1.  0-5 years
         7         2.  5-10 years
        13         3.  More than 10 years

         3         9.  NA
       191         0.  INAP., coded 5 or 9 in REF. NO. 20, or held no
                       position at this level  *Blank*
```

THE ILLINOIS LOBBYIST SURVEY   PAGE   17

VAR 0025   REF 0025   DATA SET ID-'7283'
   NAME-XTYPE ST LGSLT POS HELD   MD=0
      LOC   43 WIDTH 1   DK 1 COL 45

               Type of position -- State Legislature.
               ....
               <For the full question text of this variable see Ref. No. 21>

               SEE NOTE(S) 1

         10   1. Elected
          5   2. Appointed

        214   0. INAP., coded 5 or 9 in REF. NO. 20, or held no
                     office at this level   *Blank*

VAR 0026   REF 0026   DATA SET ID-'7283'
   NAME-XTENURE ST LGSLT POS   MD=0 OR GE 9
      LOC   44 WIDTH 1   DK 1 COL 46

               Length of tenure -- State Legislature.
               ....
               <For the full question text of this variable see Ref. No. 21>

               SEE NOTE(S) 1

          5   1. 0-5 years
          3   2. 5-10 years
          5   3. More than 10 years

          2   9. NA
        214   0. INAP., coded 5 or 9 in REF. NO. 20, or held no
                     office at this level   *Blank*

VAR 0027   REF 0027   DATA SET ID-'7283'
   NAME-XTYPE ST EXCTV POS HELD   MD=0 OR GE 9
      LOC   45 WIDTH 1   DK 1 COL 47

               Type of position -- State Executive Agency.
               ....

THE ILLINOIS LOBBYIST SURVEY

(CONTINUED)
....

<For the full question text of this variable see Ref. No. 21>

SEE NOTE(S) 1

```
      6       1. Elected
     36       2. Appointed
      1       3. Both

      1       9. NA
    185       0. INAP., coded 5 or 9 in REF. NO. 20, or held no
                 office at this level  *Blank*
```

VAR 0028   REF 0028   DATA SET ID-'7283'
    NAME-XTENURE ST EXCTV POS   MD=0 OR GE 9
    LOC   46 WIDTH 1   DK 1 COL 48

Length of tenure -- State Executive Agency.
....

<For the full question text of this variable see Ref. No. 21>

SEE NOTE(S) 1

```
     23       1. 0-5 years
     12       2. 5-10 years
      7       3. More than 10 years

      2       9. NA
    185       0. INAP., coded 5 or 9 in REF. NO. 20, or held no
                 office at this level  *Blank*
```

VAR 0029   REF 0029   DATA SET ID-'7283'
    NAME-XTYPE FDRL EXCTV POS   MD=0
    LOC   47 WIDTH 1   DK 1 COL 49

Type of position -- Federal Executive Agency.
....

<For the full question text of this variable see Ref. No. 21>

THE ILLINOIS LOBBYIST SURVEY

(CONTINUED)
....

SEE NOTE(S) 1

```
      0        1.  Elected
     13        2.  Appointed
    216        0.  INAP., coded 5 or 9 in REF. NO. 20, or held no
                   office at this level   *Blank*
```

VAR 0030   REF 0030   DATA SET ID-'7283'
   NAME-XTENURE FDRL EXCTV POS   MD=0
      LOC   48 WIDTH 1   DK 1 COL 50

Length of tenure -- Federal Executive Agency.
....
<For the full question text of this variable see Ref. No. 21>

SEE NOTE(S) 1

```
      6        1.  0-5 years
      1        2.  5-10 years
      6        3.  More than 10 years
    216        0.  INAP., coded 5 or 9 in REF. NO. 20, or held no
                   office at this level   *Blank*
```

VAR 0031   REF 0031   DATA SET ID-'7283'
   NAME-XTYPE CNGSL POS HELD   MD=0
      LOC   49 WIDTH 1   DK 1 COL 51

Type of position -- U.S. Congress.
....
<For the full question text of this variable see Ref. No. 21>

SEE NOTE(S) 1

```
      0        1.  Elected
      2        2.  Appointed
    227        0.  INAP.,coded 5 or 9 in REF. NO. 20, or held no
                   office at this level   *Blank*
```

THE ILLINOIS LOBBYIST SURVEY

VAR 0032
NAME-XTENURE CNGSL POS
LOC   50 WIDTH   1
REF 0032
MD=0 OR GE 9
DK   1 COL 52
DATA SET ID-'7283'

Length of tenure -- U.S. Congress.
....
<For the full question text of this variable see Ref. No. 21>

SEE NOTE(S) 1

```
  1       1.  0-5 years
  0       2.  5-10 years
  0       3.  More than 10 years
  1       9.  NA
227       0.  INAP., coded 5 or 9 in REF. NO. 20, or held no
              office at this level  *Blank*
```

VAR 0033
NAME-FAM MBR HELD PUB OFC
LOC   51 WIDTH   1
REF 0033
MD=GE 9
DK   1 COL 53
DATA SET ID-'7283'

A11. Have any members of your immediate family ever held public office.
....

```
 36       1.  Yes
182       5.  No
 11       9.  NA
```

VAR 0034
NAME-PARTY ID
LOC   52 WIDTH   1
REF 0034
MD=GE 4
DK   1 COL 54
DATA SET ID-'7283'

A12. Are you a: Republican, Democrat, Independent, Other.
....

SEE NOTE(S) 1

```
126       1.  Republican
```

THE ILLINOIS LOBBYIST SURVEY

(CONTINUED)

```
       68       2.  Democratic
       24       3.  Independent

        1       4.  Other
       10       9.  NA
```

VAR 0035   REF 0035   DATA SET ID-'7283'
  NAME-HELD PARTY OFFICE   MD=GE 9
  LOC   53 WIDTH 1   DK 1 COL 55

A12a. Have you ever: Held an office in a political party.

```
       57       1.  Yes
      163       5.  No

        9       9.  NA
```

VAR 0036   REF 0036   DATA SET ID-'7283'
  NAME-CONTRIBUTION TO PARTY   MD=GE 9
  LOC   54 WIDTH 1   DK 1 COL 56

A12a. <Have you ever:> Made a financial contribution to a political party.

```
      191       1.  Yes
       30       5.  No

        8       9.  NA
```

VAR 0037   REF 0037   DATA SET ID-'7283'
  NAME-INCOME   MD=GE 9
  LOC   55 WIDTH 1   DK 1 COL 57

A13. Into which of the following categories would your average yearly income fall.

SEE NOTE(S) 1

THE ILLINOIS LOBBYIST SURVEY

(CONTINUED)

6	1.	Less than $5,000
27	2.	$5,000 to $9,999
74	3.	$10,000 to $14,999
43	4.	$15,000 to $19,999
32	5.	$20,000 to $24,999
40	6.	Over $25,000
7	9.	NA

VAR 0038   REF 0038   DATA SET ID-'7283'
    NAME-% INC FROM LOBBYING   MD=GE 9
    LOC 56 WIDTH 1   DK 1 COL 58

A14. Approximately what percentage of your income is derived from your work as a legislative agent.

SEE NOTE(S) 1

13	1.	Over 75%
6	2.	50-75%
12	3.	25-50%
120	4.	Less than 25%
48	5.	None
30	9.	NA

VAR 0039   REF 0039   DATA SET ID-'7283'
    NAME-HOW LONG LOBBYIST   MD=GE 9
    LOC 57 WIDTH 1   DK 1 COL 59

A15. Approximately how long have you been a legislative agent. (Years)

17	1.	Over 20 years
23	2.	16-20 years
24	3.	11-15 years
62	4.	6-10 years
64	5.	2-5 years
25	6.	Less than 2 years

THE ILLINOIS LOBBYIST SURVEY   PAGE 23

                    (CONTINUED)
                    ....

            14   9. NA

VAR 0040   REF 0040   DATA SET ID-'7283'
   NAME-NMBR OF GRPS RPSTD 1963   NO MISSING DATA CODES
        LOC   58 WIDTH 1   DK 1 COL 60

                Number of groups R represented in the 1963 session.
                ....

           183   1. One
            36   2. Two
             8   3. Three
             0   4. Four
             2   5. Five

VAR 0041   REF 0041   DATA SET ID-'7283'
   NAME-TYPES OF GRPS RPSTD BY R   MD=GE 90   MULT RESPS 3
        LOC   59 WIDTH 2   DK 1 COL 61-66

                Types of groups R represents <three types were coded:
                First, Second, and Third, respectively>.
                ....

             2   00. Veterans' organization
            35   01. Professional organization
            16   02. Educational organization
             8   03. Agricultural organization
            26   04. Financial organization
            24   05. Labor organization
            28   06. Governmental unit
            16   07. Civic organization
            22   08. Corporation
             7   09. Religious-charitable organization
            58   10. Trade and industrial organization   *-*

             2   90. Other *&*
           443   99. NA; <or no other group represented> *Blank*

THE ILLINOIS LOBBYIST SURVEY

VAR 0042   REF 0042   DATA SET ID-'7283'
    NAME-ALWAYS RPSTD SAME GRP   MD=GE 9
    LOC   65 WIDTH 1   DK 1 COL 67

              A15a. Have you always represented the same organizations.
              ....

              187   1. Yes
               33   5. No

                9   9. NA

VAR 0043   REF 0043   DATA SET ID-'7283'
    NAME-XOTHER GRPS RPSTD BY R   MD=GE 90   MULT RESPS 4
    LOC   66 WIDTH 2   DK 1 COL 68-75

              A15b. If NO, <to REF. NO. 42> what other organizations have
              you represented.
              ....

                3   00. Veterans' organization
                7   01. Professional organization
                3   02. Educational organization
                1   03. Agricultural organization
                1   04. Financial organization
                2   05. Labor organization
                5   06. Governmental unit
                5   07. Civic organization
                9   08. Corporation
                2   09. Religious-charitable organization
                8   10. Trade and industrial organizations *-*

                1   90. Other *&*
              869   91. INAP., coded 1 or 9 in REF. NO. 42. R always
                         represented same group, or R mentions no second,
                         third, or fourth group *Blank*

VAR 0044   REF 0044   DATA SET ID-'7283'
    NAME-WILL REMAIN LBYST   MD=GE 9
    LOC   74 WIDTH 1   DK 1 COL 76

              A16. Do you plan to continue in your position as a
              legislative agent.
              ....

THE ILLINOIS LOBBYIST SURVEY

(CONTINUED)
....

```
    185     1. Yes
     29     5. No
     15     9. NA
```

VAR 0045   REF 0045   DATA SET ID-'7283'
  NAME-TIME SPNT DURING SESSION MD=GE 9
     LOC   75 WIDTH 1   DK 1 COL 77

B1. Approximately how much of your time do you spend working as a legislative agent during the legislative session.
....

SEE NOTE(S) 1

```
     30     1. Full time
     19     2. 3/4 time
     33     3. Half time
    136     4. Less than half time

     11     9. NA
```

VAR 0046   REF 0046   DATA SET ID-'7283'
  NAME-TIME SPNT BTWN SESSIONS   MD=GE 9
     LOC   76 WIDTH 1   DK 1 COL 78

B1a. Approximately how much of your time do you spend working as a legislative agent between the legislative sessions.
....

SEE NOTE(S) 1

```
      3     1. Full time
      4     2. 3/4 time
      8     3. Half time
    181     4. Less than half time
      7     5. None

     26     9. NA
```

THE ILLINOIS LOBBYIST SURVEY   PAGE 26

VAR 0047   REF 0047   DATA SET ID-'7283'
    NAME-WHY LBYST-1ST REASON   MD=0 OR GE 9
    LOC   77 WIDTH 1   DK 1 COL 79

           B2. Which of the following best describes why you became a
           legislative agent. (Please rank your reasons: (1) for the
           primary reason (2) for the second reason and (3) for the
           third)

           First reason R became a legislative agent.
           ....

                  SEE NOTE(S) 1

            163   1. The duties of my job led me into this field
             15   2. My boss felt that I was especially qualified
              3   3. I felt this was the best way for me to move up
             29   4. I wanted to promote certain policies
              6   5. The monetary reward was attractive
              1   6. Enjoys it

              1   0. Other
             11   9. NA

VAR 0048   REF 0048   DATA SET ID-'7283'
    NAME-WHY LBYST-2ND REASON   MD=0 OR GE 9
    LOC   78 WIDTH 1   DK 1 COL 80

           Second reason R became a legislative agent.
           ....

           <For the full question text of this variable see Ref. No. 47>

                  SEE NOTE(S) 1

             26   1. The duties of my job led me into this field
             17   2. My boss felt that I was especially qualified
              5   3. I felt this was the best way for me to move up
             63   4. I wanted to promote certain policies
              5   5. The monetary reward was attractive
              0   6. Enjoys it

              1   0. Other
            112   9. NA

THE ILLINOIS LOBBYIST SURVEY   PAGE 27

VAR 0001   REF 0001   DATA SET ID-'7283'
    NAME-STUDY NUMBER   NO MISSING DATA CODES
    LOC   1 WIDTH 4   DK 2 COL 1- 4

        Study Identification (7283)
        ....

        '02'   DK 2 COL 5- 6
        ....

VAR 0002   REF 0002   DATA SET ID-'7283'
    NAME-INTERVIEW NUMBER   NO MISSING DATA CODES
    LOC   5 WIDTH 3   DK 2 COL 7- 9

        Interview Number
        ....

VAR 0049   REF 0049   DATA SET ID-'7283'
    NAME-WHY LBYST-3RD REASON   MD=0 OR GE 9
    LOC   79 WIDTH 1   DK 2 COL 10

        Third reason R became a legislative agent.
        ....
        <For the full question text of this variable see Ref. No. 47>

        SEE NOTE(S) 1

            2   1. The duties of my job led me into this field
           13   2. My boss felt that I was especially qualified
           10   3. I felt this was the best way for me to move up
            7   4. I wanted to promote certain policies
            8   5. The monetary reward was attractive
            2   6. Enjoys it

           10   0. Other
          177   9. NA

DECK 2

THE ILLINOIS LOBBYIST SURVEY   PAGE 28

VAR 0050   REF 0050   DATA SET ID-'7283'
  NAME-ASPECT OF WRK LKD 1ST   MD=GE 90
    LOC   80 WIDTH 2   DK   2 COL 11-12

         B3. What are some of the aspects of your work as legis-
         lative agent that you like most. (Please rank your
         first three choices.)

         Aspect of work R likes most.
         ....

                SEE NOTE(S) 1

         28   01. The opportunity to meet people
        132   02. The opportunity to present my side of the case
          2   03. The opportunity to be close to important people
         14   04. The variety of work
          4   05. The freedom of schedule I enjoy
          6   06. The monetary reward
          0   07. Entertaining and attending parties
          9   08. Legislative activity
          2   09. No aspect more than any other   *0*

          5   90. Other *-*
         27   99. NA *9*

VAR 0051   REF 0051   DATA SET ID-'7283'
  NAME-ASPECT OF WRK LKD 2ND   MD=GE 90
    LOC   82 WIDTH 2   DK   2 COL 13-14

         Aspect of work R likes second.
         ....

         <For the full question text of this variable see Ref. No. 50>

                SEE NOTE(S) 1

         67   01. The opportunity to meet people
         20   02. The opportunity to present my side of the case
          8   03. The opportunity to be close to important people
         39   04. The variety of work
          2   05. The freedom of schedule I enjoy
          2   06. The monetary reward
          0   07. Entertaining and attending parties
          3   08. Legislative activity

THE ILLINOIS LOBBYIST SURVEY   PAGE 29

            (CONTINUED)
            ....

        2   09. No aspect more than any other   *0*
        4   90. Other   *-*
       82   99. NA

VAR 0052   REF 0052   DATA SET ID-'7283'
   NAME-ASPECT OF WRK LKD 3RD   MD=GE 90
       LOC   84 WIDTH 2   DK 2 COL 15-16

       Aspect of work R likes third.
       ....
       <For the full question text of this variable see Ref. No. 50>

            SEE NOTE(S) 1

       27   01. The opportunity to meet people
       12   02. The opportunity to present my side of the case
       12   03. The opportunity to be close to important people
       36   04. The variety of work
       13   05. The freedom of schedule I enjoy
        1   06. The monetary reward
        4   07. Entertaining and attending parties
        1   08. Legislative activity
        2   09. No aspect more than any other   *0*

       11   90. Other   *-*
      110   99. NA   *9*

VAR 0053   REF 0053   DATA SET ID-'7283'
   NAME-ASPECT LIKED LEAST 1ST   MD=GE 8
       LOC   86 WIDTH 1   DK 2 COL 17

       B4. What are some of the aspects of your work that you find
       least appealing. (Please rank your choices: (1) for the
       least appealing, (2) for the second least, and (3) for the
       third).

       Aspect of work R finds least appealing.
       ....

            SEE NOTE(S) 1

THE ILLINOIS LOBBYIST SURVEY

(CONTINUED)

22	0.	No aspect liked least
2	1.	I dislike preparing a case to present
52	2.	I dislike the necessity of being nice to people in order to get their help
21	3.	I dislike the working conditions and the long hours
23	4.	I dislike the possible discouragement through failure
36	5.	I dislike the public image of my job
16	6.	I dislike entertaining and giving parties
9	7.	Morals and activities of legislators *8*
9	8.	Other *7*
39	9.	NA *9*

VAR 0054　　　　　　　　　　REF 0054　　　　　　　　DATA SET ID-'7283'
　　NAME-ASPECT LIKED LEAST 2ND　　MD=GE 8
　　　　LOC　87 WIDTH　1　　　DK　2 COL 18

Aspect of work R likes second least.

<For the full question text of this variable see Ref. No. 53>

SEE NOTE(S) 1

25	0.	No aspect liked <second> least
3	1.	I dislike preparing a case to present
21	2.	I dislike the necessity of being nice to people in order to get their help
22	3.	I dislike the working conditions and the long hours
21	4.	I dislike the possible discouragement through failure
21	5.	I dislike the public image of my job
13	6.	I dislike entertaining and giving parties
7	7.	Morals and activities of legislators *8*
3	8.	Other *7*
93	9.	NA *9*

THE ILLINOIS LOBBYIST SURVEY

VAR 0055   REF 0055   DATA SET ID-'7283'
  NAME-ASPECT LIKED LEAST 3RD   MD=GE 8
     LOC   88 WIDTH   1   DK 2 COL 19

          Aspect of work R likes third least.
          ....
          <For the full question text of this variable see Ref. No. 53>

          SEE NOTE(S) 1

      25   0. No aspect liked <third> least
       6   1. I dislike preparing a case to present
      13   2. I dislike the necessity of being nice to people in
                 order to get their help
       8   3. I dislike the working conditions and the long hours
      16   4. I dislike the possible discouragement through
                 failure
      15   5. I dislike the public image of my job
      12   6. I dislike entertaining and giving parties
       5   7. Morals and activities of legislators *8*

       4   8. Other *7*
     125   9. NA *9*

VAR 0056   REF 0056   DATA SET ID-'7283'
  NAME-LBYST MOST NEEDED QLTY   MD=GE 9
     LOC   89 WIDTH   1   DK 2 COL 20

          B5. From your experience what qualities do you think are
          most important for a legislative agent. (Please rank your
          choices (1) for that quality most important, (2) for the
          second, etc.)

          Most important quality.
          ....

          SEE NOTE(S) 1

      55   1. A previous knowledge of the Illinois legislature and
                 its inner workings
      22   2. The ability to talk and persuade other people
      92   3. A knowledge of the subject matter my organization
                 is interested in
      26   4. The possession of a wide circle of friends in state

THE ILLINOIS LOBBYIST SURVEY

(CONTINUED)
....

```
                  government
        1     5.  The ability to compromise
        1     6.  The willingness to work
        1     7.  Ability to bring pressure
        9     8.  Honesty

       22     9.  NA
```

VAR 0057   REF 0057   DATA SET ID-'7283'
NAME-MOST NEEDED QLTY 2ND   MD=GE 9
    LOC   90 WIDTH 1   DK 2 COL 21

Second most important quality <for a lobbyist>.
....
<For the full question text of this variable see Ref. No. 56>

```
              SEE NOTE(S) 1

       50     1.  A previous knowledge of the Illinois legislature and
                  its inner workings
       49     2.  The ability to talk and persuade other people
       56     3.  A knowledge of the subject matter my organization
                  is interested in
       29     4.  The possession of a wide circle of friends in state
                  government
        0     5.  The ability to compromise
        0     6.  The willingness to work
        0     7.  Ability to bring pressure
        4     8.  Honesty

       41     9.  NA
```

VAR 0058   REF 0058   DATA SET ID-'7283'
NAME-MOST NEEDED QLTY 3RD   MD=0 OR GE 9
    LOC   91 WIDTH 1   DK 2 COL 22

Third most important quality <for a lobbyist>.
....
<For the full question text of this variable see Ref. No. 56>

THE ILLINOIS LOBBYIST SURVEY   PAGE   33

                (CONTINUED)
                ....

                SEE NOTE(S) 1

        36   1. A previous knowledge of the Illinois legislature and
                    its inner workings
        67   2. The ability to talk and persuade other people
        28   3. A knowledge of the subject matter my organization
                    is interested in
        24   4. The possession of a wide circle of friends in state
                    government
         0   5. The ability to compromise
         0   6. The willingness to work
         1   7. Ability to bring pressure
         0   8. Honesty

         1   0. Other
        72   9. NA

VAR 0059   REF 0059   DATA SET ID-'7283'
   NAME-LBYST MAJOR WORK 1ST   MD=GE 7
        LOC 92 WIDTH 1   DK 2 COL 23

        B6. As a legislative agent for your organization,
        does your work involve mainly: (if more than one answer
        is appropriate please rank your responses)

        Major type of work involved in as a lobbyist.
        ....

                SEE NOTE(S) 1

        38   1. Appearing before a legislative committee
        65   2. Talking with legislators
         7   3. Talking with officials of state agencies
        55   4. Keeping my organization informed of happenings in
                    Springfield
         4   5. Prepare testimony, plan strategy, etc.   *7*
        41   6. Indicated all or some but did not rank

         2   7. Other   *5*
        17   9. NA

THE ILLINOIS LOBBYIST SURVEY

VAR 0060   REF 0060   DATA SET ID-'7283'
   NAME-LBYST MAJOR WORK 2ND   MD=GE 7
      LOC 93 WIDTH 1   DK 2 COL 24

Second type of work involved in as lobbyist.
....
<For the full question text of this variable see Ref. No. 59>

SEE NOTE(S) 1

62	1. Appearing before a legislative committee
49	2. Talking with legislators
6	3. Talking with officials of state agencies
32	4. Keeping my organization informed of happenings in Springfield
2	5. Prepare testimony, plan strategy, etc. *7*
36	6. Indicated all or some but did not rank
1	7. Other *5*
41	9. NA

VAR 0061   REF 0061   DATA SET ID-'7283'
   NAME-LBYST MAJOR WORK 3RD   MD=GE 7
      LOC 94 WIDTH 1   DK 2 COL 25

Third type of work involved in as lobbyist.
....
<For the full question text of this variable see Ref. No. 59>

SEE NOTE(S) 1

23	1. Appearing before a legislative committee
25	2. Talking with legislators
31	3. Talking with officials of state agencies
35	4. Keeping my organization informed of happenings in Springfield
0	5. Prepare testimony, plan strategy, etc. *7*
37	6. Indicated all or some but did not rank
1	7. Other *5*
77	9. NA

THE ILLINOIS LOBBYIST SURVEY

VAR 0062   REF 0062   DATA SET ID-'7283'
   NAME-ACTVY EXPECTED TO DO 1ST   MD=GE 90
      LOC   95 WIDTH 2   DK 2 COL 26-27

B7. In your work as a legislative agent you engage
in different kinds of activities. Perhaps some of these
activities are expected by your organization, some
will be more difficult to perform, and in some activities
you probably have more success than in others. Below are
listed certain possible activities, in each column
(expected, most difficult, and most success) would you rank
the top three activities which your organization expects
you to perform, those most difficult to perform, and those at
which you feel you are most successful.

Activity R is first expected to perform.
....

SEE NOTE(S) 1

```
   55         01. Prevent the passage of harmful legislation
   33         02. Secure the passage of favorable legislation
    1         03. Secure minor changes in legislation, i.e., wording
   18         04. Present the views of my organization
    3         05. Maintain friendly relations with officials
    2         06. Aid individual organizational members
    1         07. Report back   *8*
   67         08. Did not rank but indicated number 1  *0*
   10         09. Did not rank but indicated number 2  *-*
    3         10. Did not rank but indicated number 3  *&*

    0         90. Other   *7*
   36         99. NA  *9*
```

VAR 0063   REF 0063   DATA SET ID-'7283'
   NAME-ACTVY EXPECTED TO DO 2ND   MD=GE 90
      LOC   97 WIDTH 2   DK 2 COL 28-29

Activity R is expected to perform second.
....
<For the full question text of this variable see Ref. No. 62>

SEE NOTE(S) 1

THE ILLINOIS LOBBYIST SURVEY

(CONTINUED)

Count	Code	Description
28	01.	Prevent the passage of harmful legislation
42	02.	Secure the passage of favorable legislation
8	03.	Secure minor changes in legislation, i.e., wording
12	04.	Present the views of my organization
5	05.	Maintain friendly relations with officials
3	06.	Aid individual organizational members
0	07.	Report back *8*
0	08.	Did not rank but indicated number 1 *0*
50	09.	Did not rank but indicated number 2 *-*
9	10.	Did not rank but indicated number 3 *&*
0	90.	Other *7*
72	99.	NA *9*

VAR 0064   REF 0064   DATA SET ID-'7283'
   NAME-ACTVY EXPECTED TO DO 3RD   MD=GE 90
      LOC   99 WIDTH 2   DK 2 COL 30-31

Third activity R is expected to perform.

<For the full question text of this variable see Ref. No. 62>

SEE NOTE(S) 1

Count	Code	Description
9	01.	Prevent the passage of harmful legislation
10	02.	Secure the passage of favorable legislation
21	03.	Secure minor changes in legislation, i.e., wording
32	04.	Present the views of my organization
12	05.	Maintain friendly relations with officials
4	06.	Aid individual organizational members
0	07.	Report back *8*
0	08.	Did not rank but indicated number 1 *0*
0	09.	Did not rank but indicated number 2 *-*
28	10.	Did not rank but indicated number 3 *&*
0	90.	Other *7*
113	99.	NA *9*

THE ILLINOIS LOBBYIST SURVEY   PAGE   37

VAR 0065   REF 0065   DATA SET ID-'7283'
     NAME-ACTVY MOST DFCLT 1ST   MD=GE 90
     LOC   101 WIDTH   2   DK   2 COL 32-33

                Activity R ranked as most difficult to perform.
                ....
                <For the full question text of this variable see Ref. No. 62>

                SEE NOTE(S) 1

         37   01. Prevent the passage of harmful legislation
         98   02. Secure the passage of favorable legislation
          2   03. Secure minor changes in legislation, i.e., wording
          2   04. Present the views of my organization
          2   05. Maintain friendly relations with officials
          6   06. Aid individual organizational members
          0   07. Report back   *8*
         13   08. Did not rank but indicated number 1 *0*
          5   09. Did not rank but indicated number 2 *-*
          1   10. Did not rank but indicated number 3 *&*

          1   90. Other   *7*
         62   99. NA   *9*

VAR 0066   REF 0066   DATA SET ID-'7283'
     NAME-ACTVY MOST DFCLT 2ND   MD=GE 90
     LOC   103 WIDTH   2   DK   2 COL 34-35

                Activity R ranked as second most difficult to perform.
                ....
                <For the full question text of this variable see Ref. No. 62>

                SEE NOTE(S) 1

         33   01. Prevent the passage of harmful legislation
         11   02. Secure the passage of favorable legislation
         13   03. Secure minor changes in legislation, i.e., wording
          8   04. Present the views of my organization
          0   05. Maintain friendly relations with officials
          5   06. Aid individual organizational members
          0   07. Report back   *8*
          0   08. Did not rank but indicated number 1 *0*
         12   09. Did not rank but indicated number 2 *-*

THE ILLINOIS LOBBYIST SURVEY   PAGE 38

                (CONTINUED)
                ....

        4   10. Did not rank but indicated number 3 *&*
        0   90. Other   *7*
      143   99. NA   *9*

VAR 0067   REF 0067   DATA SET ID-'7283'
   NAME-ACTVY MOST DFCLT 3RD   MD=GE 90
   LOC 105 WIDTH 2   DK 2 COL 36-37

           Activity R ranked as third most difficult to perform.
           ....
           <For the full question text of this variable see Ref. No. 62>

                SEE NOTE(S) 1

       14   01. Prevent the passage of harmful legislation
        5   02. Secure the passage of favorable legislation
       18   03. Secure minor changes in legislation, i.e., wording
       18   04. Present the views of my organization
        7   05. Maintain friendly relations with officials
        1   06. Aid individual organizational members
        0   07. Report back *8*
        0   08. Did not rank but indicated number 1 *0*
        0   09. Did not rank but indicated number 2 *-*
        3   10. Did not rank but indicated number 3 *&*

        0   90. Other   *7*
      163   99. NA   *9*

VAR 0068   REF 0068   DATA SET ID-'7283'
   NAME-ACTVY MOST SUCCESS 1ST   MD=GE 90
   LOC 107 WIDTH 2   DK 2 COL 38-39

           Activity R has the most success at performing.
           ....
           <For the full question text of this variable see Ref. No. 62>

                SEE NOTE(S) 1

       49   01. Prevent the passage of harmful legislation

THE ILLINOIS LOBBYIST SURVEY   PAGE 39

              (CONTINUED)
              ....

          17   02. Secure the passage of favorable legislation
          25   03. Secure minor changes in legislation, i.e., wording
          28   04. Present the views of my organization
          10   05. Maintain friendly relations with officials
           1   06. Aid individual organizational members
           1   07. Report back *8*
          39   08. Did not rank but indicated number 1 *0*
          10   09. Did not rank but indicated number 2 *-*
           4   10. Did not rank but indicated number 3 *&*

           0   90. Other *7*
          45   99. NA *9*

VAR 0069   REF 0069   DATA SET ID-'7283'
   NAME-ACTVY MOST SUCCESS 2ND   MD=GE 90
      LOC 109 WIDTH 2   DK 2 COL 40-41

              Activity R has second most success at performing.
              ....

              <For the full question text of this variable see Ref. No. 62>

              SEE NOTE(S) 1

          22   01. Prevent the passage of harmful legislation
          16   02. Secure the passage of favorable legislation
          14   03. Secure minor changes in legislation, i.e., wording
          15   04. Present the views of my organization
          14   05. Maintain friendly relations with officials
           2   06. Aid individual organizational members
           0   07. Report back *8*
           0   08. Did not rank but indicated number 1 *0*
          13   09. Did not rank but indicated number 2 *-*
          23   10. Did not rank but indicated number 3 *&*

           0   90. Other *7*
         110   99. NA *9*

VAR 0070   REF 0070   DATA SET ID-'7283'
   NAME-ACTVY MOST SUCCESS 3RD   MD=GE 90
      LOC 111 WIDTH 2   DK 2 COL 42-43

              Activity R has third most success at performing.
              ....

THE ILLINOIS LOBBYIST SURVEY

(CONTINUED)
....

<For the full question text of this variable see Ref. No. 62>

SEE NOTE(S) 1

17	01.	Prevent the passage of harmful legislation
24	02.	Secure the passage of favorable legislation
19	03.	Secure minor changes in legislation, i.e., wording
9	04.	Present the views of my organization
3	05.	Maintain friendly relations with officials
1	06.	Aid individual organizational members
0	07.	Report back *8*
0	08.	Did not rank but indicated number 1 *0*
0	09.	Did not rank but indicated number 2 *-*
6	10.	Did not rank but indicated number 3 *&*
0	90.	Other *7*
150	99.	NA *9*

```
VAR 0071                    REF 0071                DATA SET ID-'7283'
  NAME-NMBR LGSLTRS TLKD TO    MD=GE 9
      LOC 113 WIDTH 1          DK 2 COL 44
```

B8. Approximately how many legislators will you talk with in person during a session.
....

SEE NOTE(S) 1

26	1.	Over 175
7	2.	150-175
27	3.	125-150
23	4.	90-125
48	5.	50-90
46	6.	20-50
32	7.	5-20
8	8.	Less than 5
12	9.	NA

THE ILLINOIS LOBBYIST SURVEY   PAGE 41

VAR 0072   REF 0072   DATA SET ID-'7283'
   NAME-LGSLN YOUR GRP INTST IN   MD=GE 90
      LOC 114 WIDTH 2   DK 2 COL 45-46

           B9. What legislation was your organization interested in
           during the 1963 session.

           First choice.
           ....

              1   00. None
             27   10. Governmental legislation (pertains to local
                        government)
             38   20. Welfare -- including labor
             33   30. Taxation
             13   40. Education
             11   50. Regulatory -- professions
             42   60. Regulatory -- Other
              2   70. All *-*

             14   90. Other -- including special legislation *&*
             48   99. NA *9*

VAR 0073   REF 0073   DATA SET ID-'7283'
   NAME-LGSLN INTST IN 2ND   MD=GE 90
      LOC 116 WIDTH 2   DK 2 COL 47-48

           Second choice <of type of legislation>.
           ....
           <For the full question text of this variable see Ref. No. 72>

              0   00. None
             24   10. Governmental legislation (pertains to local
                        government)
             17   20. Welfare -- including labor
             10   30. Taxation
              2   40. Education
              1   50. Regulatory -- professions
             15   60. Regulatory -- Other
              0   70. All *-*

              6   90. Other -- including special legislation *&*
            106   92. None listed (no second choice) *Blank*
             48   99. NA *9*

THE ILLINOIS LOBBYIST SURVEY   PAGE 42

VAR 0074   REF 0074   DATA SET ID-'7283'
    NAME-LGSLN INTST IN 3RD   MD=GE 90
         LOC 118 WIDTH 2   DK 2 COL 49-50

            Third choice <of type of legislation>.
            ....
            <For the full question text of this variable see Ref. No. 72>

         0   00. None
         5   10. Governmental legislation (pertains to local
                    government)
         5   20. Welfare -- including labor
         3   30. Taxation
         2   40. Education
         0   50. Regulatory -- professions
         4   60. Regulatory -- Other
         0   70. All *-*

         6   90. Other -- including special legislation *&*
       156   92. None listed (no third choice) *Blank*
        48   99. NA *9*

VAR 0075   REF 0075   DATA SET ID-'7283'
    NAME-LGSLTR SHLD REPRESENT   MD=GE 9
         LOC 120 WIDTH 1   DK 2 COL 51

            C1. As an observer of the state legislature which one of
            the following do you believe legislators should represent
            and which one do you think they actually do represent.

            Whom does R think legislators SHOULD represent.
            ....

            SEE NOTE(S) 1

        36   1. The majority of Illinois voters
         5   2. The principles of their respective parties
        38   3. The people of their district
         3   4. The views of prominent groups (e.g., labor
         0   5. The wishes of their respective factions (e.g.,
                   Cook County)
        30   6. Their own ideas and judgments on what is best
        95   7. Combination of the above

        22   9. NA

THE ILLINOIS LOBBYIST SURVEY   PAGE 43

VAR 0076   REF 0076   DATA SET ID-'7283'
   NAME-LGSLTR DO REPRESENT   MD=GE 9
      LOC 121 WIDTH 1   DK 2 COL 52

         Whom does R think legislators DO represent.
         ....

              SEE NOTE(S) 1

          2   1. The majority of Illinois voters
         19   2. The principles of their respective parties
         24   3. The people of their district
         18   4. The views of prominent groups (e.g., labor
         32   5. The wishes of their respective factions (e.g.,
                    Cook County)
         11   6. Their own ideas and judgments on what is best
        104   7. Combination of the above

         19   9. NA

VAR 0077   REF 0077   DATA SET ID-'7283'
   NAME-WHERE CNCTRT ACTVY 1ST   MD=GE 99
      LOC 122 WIDTH 2   DK 2 COL 53-54

         C2. From your experience at which points in the legislative
         process do you concentrate your activity as a legislative
         agent. (Please rank your first three choices)

         First choice.
         ....

              SEE NOTE(S) 1

         36   01. Before a bill is introduced
         13   02. Before a bill is assigned to a committee
         68   03. During the time of committee hearings
         22   04. Just prior to a committee vote
          1   05. After the bill is returned to the floor
          0   06. During the floor debate on the bill
          0   07. Floor vote   *0*
          2   08. Prior to hearing but after assignment *-*
         31   09. Activity varies too much with each bill *8*
         20   10. Cannot differentiate activity between the various
                   periods   *7*

THE ILLINOIS LOBBYIST SURVEY   PAGE 44

                (CONTINUED)
                ....
            36   99. NA *9*

VAR 0078   REF 0078   DATA SET ID-'7283'
    NAME-WHERE CNCTRT ACTVY 2ND   MD=GE 99
        LOC 124 WIDTH 2   DK 2 COL 55-56

                Second choice <of where R concentrates activity>.
                ....
                <For the full question text of this variable see Ref. No. 77>

                SEE NOTE(S) 1

            13   01. Before a bill is introduced
            19   02. Before a bill is assigned to a committee
            48   03. During the time of committee hearings
            35   04. Just prior to a committee vote
            18   05. After the bill is returned to the floor
             3   06. During the floor debate on the bill
             0   07. Floor vote *0*
             0   08. Prior to hearing but after assignment *-*
            18   09. Activity varies too much with each bill *8*
            12   10. Cannot differentiate activity between the various
                        periods *7*

            63   99. NA *9*

VAR 0079   REF 0079   DATA SET ID-'7283'
    NAME-WHERE CNCTRT ACTVY 3RD   MD=GE 99
        LOC 126 WIDTH 2   DK 2 COL 57-58

                Third choice <of where R concentrates activity>.
                ....
                <For the full question text of this variable see Ref. No. 77>

                SEE NOTE(S) 1

            12   01. Before a bill is introduced
             7   02. Before a bill is assigned to a committee
            17   03. During the time of committee hearings
            19   04. Just prior to a committee vote

THE ILLINOIS LOBBYIST SURVEY

(CONTINUED)

```
40      05. After the bill is returned to the floor
19      06. During the floor debate on the bill
 1      07. Floor vote  *0*
 0      08. Prior to hearing but after assignment  *-*
25      09. Activity varies too much with each bill  *8*
 6      10. Cannot differentiate activity between the various
            periods  *7*

83      99. NA  *9*
```

VAR 0080   REF 0080   DATA SET ID-'7283'
NAME-WRK MUCH WITH BOTH PTY   MD=GE 9
    LOC 128 WIDTH 1   DK 2 COL 59

C3. To what extent do you work with both Republican and Democratic legislators.

SEE NOTE(S) 1

```
142     1. Always
 47     2. Frequently
 19     3. Occasionally
  9     4. Seldom
  1     5. Never

 11     9. NA
```

VAR 0081   REF 0081   DATA SET ID-'7283'
NAME-EFCTVS-PSNL VIEWPOINT   MD=GE 9
    LOC 129 WIDTH 1   DK 2 COL 60

C4. Here are some factors that are thought to be important for a legislative agent to do in order to be most effective in his work. From your experience how effective do you think each of the following activities is in furthering the goals of your organization in the Illinois General Assembly. (Please indicate the effectiveness for each response)

Personal presentation of organization's view - Effectiveness.

THE ILLINOIS LOBBYIST SURVEY   PAGE 46

           (CONTINUED)
           ....

           SEE NOTE(S) 1

     107   1. Very
      58   2. Fairly
      31   3. Some
      14   4. Little
       0   5. Not at all

      19   9. NA

VAR 0082   REF 0082   DATA SET ID-'7283'
   NAME-EFCTVS-RESEARCH   MD=GE 9
   LOC 130 WIDTH 1   DK 2 COL 61

           Presentation of research results - Effectiveness.
           ....
           <For the full question text of this variable see Ref. No. 81>

           SEE NOTE(S) 1

      55   1. Very
      52   2. Fairly
      67   3. Some
      26   4. Little
       0   5. Not at all

      29   9. NA

VAR 0083   REF 0083   DATA SET ID-'7283'
   NAME-EFCTVS-COMMITTEE TSTMNY   MD=GE 9
   LOC 131 WIDTH 1   DK 2 COL 62

           Testifying at hearings - Effectiveness.
           ....
           <For the full question text of this variable see Ref. No. 81>

           SEE NOTE(S) 1

      78   1. Very
      67   2. Fairly

THE ILLINOIS LOBBYIST SURVEY

(CONTINUED)
....

42	3. Some
20	4. Little
0	5. Not at all
22	9. NA

VAR 0084 REF 0084 DATA SET ID-'7283'
NAME-EFCTVS-CNST CONTACT   MD=GE 9
LOC 132 WIDTH 1   DK 2 COL 63

Personal contact with officials by constituents - Effectiveness.
....
<For the full question text of this variable see Ref. No. 81>

SEE NOTE(S) 1

131	1. Very
42	2. Fairly
29	3. Some
7	4. Little
1	5. Not at all
19	9. NA

VAR 0085 REF 0085 DATA SET ID-'7283'
NAME-EFCTVS-CNTCT BY FRIENDS   MD=GE 9
LOC 133 WIDTH 1   DK 2 COL 64

Personal contact with officials by close friends - Effectiveness.
....
<For the full question text of this variable see Ref. No. 81>

SEE NOTE(S) 1

102	1. Very
46	2. Fairly
29	3. Some
17	4. Little

THE ILLINOIS LOBBYIST SURVEY   PAGE 48

              (CONTINUED)
              ....

         2   5. Not at all
        33   9. NA

VAR 0086   REF 0086   DATA SET ID-'7283'
    NAME-EFCTVS-LTR-TLGRM CMPN   MD=GE 9
    LOC 134 WIDTH 1   DK 2 COL 65

              Letter and Telegram campaigns - Effectiveness.
              ....
              <For the full question text of this variable see Ref. No. 81>

              SEE NOTE(S) 1

        42   1. Very
        57   2. Fairly
        54   3. Some
        42   4. Little
        11   5. Not at all

        23   9. NA

VAR 0087   REF 0087   DATA SET ID-'7283'
    NAME-EFCTVS-P.R CAMPAIGN   MD=GE 9
    LOC 135 WIDTH 1   DK 2 COL 66

              Public relations campaign - Effectiveness.
              ....
              <For the full question text of this variable see Ref. No. 81>

              SEE NOTE(S) 1

        24   1. Very
        33   2. Fairly
        78   3. Some
        53   4. Little
         9   5. Not at all

        32   9. NA

THE ILLINOIS LOBBYIST SURVEY

VAR 0088
NAME-EFCTVS-VOTING RECORD
LOC 136 WIDTH 1

REF 0088
MD=GE 9
DK 2 COL 67

DATA SET ID-'7283'

Publicizing voting record - Effectiveness.
....

<For the full question text of this variable see Ref. No. 81>

SEE NOTE(S) 1

17	1. Very
36	2. Fairly
43	3. Some
69	4. Little
35	5. Not at all
29	9. NA

VAR 0089
NAME-EFCTVS-ENTERTAINMENT
LOC 137 WIDTH 1

REF 0089
MD=GE 9
DK 2 COL 68

DATA SET ID-'7283'

Entertaining legislators - Effectiveness.
....

<For the full question text of this variable see Ref. No. 81>

SEE NOTE(S) 1

12	1. Very
25	2. Fairly
64	3. Some
64	4. Little
29	5. Not at all
35	9. NA

THE ILLINOIS LOBBYIST SURVEY

PAGE 50

VAR 0090   REF 0090   DATA SET ID-'7283'
    NAME-EFCTVS-CAMPAIGN CNTRBS   MD=GE 9
    LOC 138 WIDTH 1   DK 2 COL 69

        Contributing money to campaigns - Effectiveness.
        ....
        <For the full question text of this variable see Ref. No. 81>

        SEE NOTE(S) 1

        61   1. Very
        44   2. Fairly
        34   3. Some
        29   4. Little
        27   5. Not at all

        34   9. NA

VAR 0091   REF 0091   DATA SET ID-'7283'
    NAME-EFCTVS-CAMPAIGN WORK   MD=0 OR GE 9
    LOC 139 WIDTH 1   DK 2 COL 70

        Campaign work - Effectiveness.
        ....
        <For the full question text of this variable see Ref. No. 81>

        4   1. Very
        0   2. Fairly
        0   3. Some
        0   4. Little
        0   5. Not at all

        0   9. NA
        225   0. R did not suggest this item *Blank*

VAR 0092   REF 0092   DATA SET ID-'7283'
    NAME-WORK WITH OTHER LBYST   MD=GE 6
    LOC 140 WIDTH 1   DK 2 COL 71

        C5. Sometimes, we are told, legislative agents work
        together on a legislative proposal. Of what importance do

THE ILLINOIS LOBBYIST SURVEY   PAGE 51

(CONTINUED)
....
you give this factor in the success of your organization.
....

SEE NOTE(S) 1

```
50      1. Most important factor
87      2. Of much importance
50      3. Of moderate importance
17      4. Of slight importance
 3      5. Of no importance

11      6. Important but not to R's group
11      9. NA
```

VAR 0093   REF 0093   DATA SET ID-'7283'
   NAME-WORK WITH PRFNL GRPS   MD=GE 5
      LOC 141 WIDTH 1   DK 2 COL 72

C6. Please rate each of the following type of organizations according to the frequency of joint effort with your group. (In answering this question use a (0) to indicate no joint efforts, (1) for occasional use of joint effort, (2) for joint effort, (3) for frequent joint effort, and (4) for constant joint effort.)

Joint effort - Professional organizations.
....

SEE NOTE(S) 1

```
45      0. <Never>
56      1. Occasional
26      2. Moderate
32      3. Frequent
20      4. Constant

 1      5. Indicated but did not rank
49      9. NA
```

THE ILLINOIS LOBBYIST SURVEY

VAR 0094   REF 0094   DATA SET ID-'7283'
    NAME-WORK WITH EDNL GROUPS   MD=GE 9
    LOC 142 WIDTH 1   DK 2 COL 73

   Joint effort - Educational organizations.
   ....
   <For the full question text of this variable see Ref. No. 93>

           SEE NOTE(S) 1

       57   0. <Never>
       56   1. Occasional
       19   2. Moderate
       19   3. Frequent
       16   4. Constant

       62   9. NA

VAR 0095   REF 0095   DATA SET ID-'7283'
    NAME-WORK WITH AGRIC GROUPS   MD=GE 5
    LOC 143 WIDTH 1   DK 2 COL 74

   Joint effort - Agricultural organizations.
   ....
   <For the full question text of this variable see Ref. No. 93>

           SEE NOTE(S) 1

       86   0. <Never>
       36   1. Occasional
       21   2. Moderate
       14   3. Frequent
        8   4. Constant

        1   5. Indicated but did not rank
       63   9. NA

THE ILLINOIS LOBBYIST SURVEY

VAR 0096   REF 0096   DATA SET ID-'7283'
   NAME-WORK WITH FINANCIAL GRPS   MD=GE 9
      LOC 144 WIDTH 1   DK 2 COL 75

   Joint effort - Financial organizations.
   ....
   <For the full question text of this variable see Ref. No. 93>

   SEE NOTE(S) 1

84	0.	<Never>
39	1.	Occasional
18	2.	Moderate
14	3.	Frequent
4	4.	Constant
70	9.	NA

VAR 0097   REF 0097   DATA SET ID-'7283'
   NAME-WORK WITH LABOR UNIONS   MD=GE 5
      LOC 145 WIDTH 1   DK 2 COL 76

   Joint effort - Labor organizations.
   ....
   <For the full question text of this variable see Ref. No. 93>

   SEE NOTE(S) 1

58	0.	<Never>
59	1.	Occasional
20	2.	Moderate
20	3.	Frequent
24	4.	Constant
1	5.	Indicated but did not rank
47	9.	NA

THE ILLINOIS LOBBYIST SURVEY

VAR 0098
    NAME-WORK WITH GOVT UNITS   REF 0098   DATA SET ID-'7283'
    LOC   146 WIDTH   1   MD=GE 9
                                    DK   2 COL 77

         Joint effort - Governmental units.
         ....

         <For the full question text of this variable see Ref. No. 93>

         SEE NOTE(S) 1

         43   0. <Never>
         42   1. Occasional
         35   2. Moderate
         43   3. Frequent
         13   4. Constant

         53   9. NA

VAR 0099
    NAME-WORK WITH CIVIC GROUPS   REF 0099   DATA SET ID-'7283'
    LOC   147 WIDTH   1   MD=GE 9
                                    DK   2 COL 78

         Joint effort - Civic organizations.
         ....

         <For the full question text of this variable see Ref. No. 93>

         SEE NOTE(S) 1

         43   0. <Never>
         47   1. Occasional
         26   2. Moderate
         41   3. Frequent
         19   4. Constant

         53   9. NA

THE ILLINOIS LOBBYIST SURVEY   PAGE 55

```
VAR 0100                        REF 0100              DATA SET ID-'7283'
    NAME-WORK WITH CORPORATIONS    MD=GE 9
    LOC   148 WIDTH   1            DK  2 COL 79
```

Joint effort - Corporations.
....

<For the full question text of this variable see Ref. No. 93>

SEE NOTE(S) 1

```
    83      0.  <Never>
    22      1.  Occasional
    18      2.  Moderate
    23      3.  Frequent
    18      4.  Constant

    65      9.  NA
```

D
E
C
K
3

```
VAR 0001                        REF 0001              DATA SET ID-'7283'
    NAME-STUDY NUMBER              NO MISSING DATA CODES
    LOC   1 WIDTH   4              DK  3 COL   1- 4
```

Study Identification (7283)
....

'03'   DK 3 COL 5- 6
....

```
VAR 0002                        REF 0002              DATA SET ID-'7283'
    NAME-INTERVIEW NUMBER          NO MISSING DATA CODES
    LOC   5 WIDTH   3              DK  3 COL   7- 9
```

Interview Number
....

```
VAR 0101                        REF 0101              DATA SET ID-'7283'
    NAME-WRK WITH RLGS-CHTBL GRPS  MD=GE 5
    LOC   149 WIDTH   1            DK  3 COL 10
```

Joint effort - Religious-Charitable <organizations>.
....

THE ILLINOIS LOBBYIST SURVEY   PAGE 56

             (CONTINUED)
             ....

             <For the full question text of this variable see Ref. No. 93

                  SEE NOTE(S) 1

             109   0. <Never>
              27   1. Occasional
              14   2. Moderate
               5   3. Frequent
               4   4. Constant

               1   5. Indicated but did not rank
              69   9. NA

VAR 0102   REF 0102   DATA SET ID-'7283'
    NAME-WORK WITH VETERANS GRPS   MD=GE 5
         LOC 150 WIDTH 1   DK 3 COL 11

             Joint effort - Veterans' organizations
             ....
             <For the full question text of this variable see Ref. No. 93>

                  SEE NOTE(S) 1

             117   0. <Never>
              26   1. Occasional
               7   2. Moderate
               3   3. Frequent
               5   4. Constant

               2   5. Indicated but did not rank
              69   9. NA

VAR 0103   REF 0103   DATA SET ID-'7283'
    NAME-WORK WITH TRD-NDSTL GRPS   MD=GE 9
         LOC 151 WIDTH 1   DK 3 COL 12

             Joint effort - Trade and Industrial associations.
             ....
             <For the full question text of this variable see Ref. No. 93>

THE ILLINOIS LOBBYIST SURVEY   PAGE 57

                (CONTINUED)
                ....

                SEE NOTE(S) 1

        50   0. <Never>
        38   1. Occasional
        21   2. Moderate
        34   3. Frequent
        38   4. Constant

        48   9. NA

VAR 0104   REF 0104   DATA SET ID-'7283'
    NAME-MOST SCSFL LOBBYING GRP   MD=GE 99
        LOC 152 WIDTH 2   DK 3 COL 13-14

                C7. Which of the following organizations do you think
                are the most successful in obtaining desired legislation.
                (Please rank (1) for the most successful, (2) for the
                next, etc.)

                Most successful organization.
                ....

                SEE NOTE(S) 1

         3   00. Veterans' organizations
        18   01. Professional organizations
        32   02. Educational
         9   03. Agricultural organizations
         8   04. Financial organizations
        35   05. Labor organizations
        38   06. Governmental units
         1   07. Civic organizations
        13   08. Corporations
         1   09. Religious-Charitable <organizations> *&*
        25   10. Trade and Industrial associations *-*

        46   99. NA *9*

VARIABLE 104

THE ILLINOIS LOBBYIST SURVEY

VAR 0105   REF 0105   DATA SET ID-'7283'
    NAME-SCSFL LOBBYING GRP 2ND   MD=GE 99
    LOC   154 WIDTH 2   DK 3 COL 15-16

              Second most successful organization.
              ....
              <For the full question text of this variable see Ref. No. 104

              SEE NOTE(S) 1

         8   00. Veterans' <organizations>
        12   01. Professional organizations
        15   02. Educational organizations
        20   03. Agricultural organizations
         7   04. Financial organizations
        43   05. Labor organizations
        21   06. Governmental units
         8   07. Civic organizations
        17   08. Corporations
         5   09. Religious-Charitable <organizations> *&*
        16   10. Trade and Industrial associations *-*

        57   99. NA *9*

VAR 0106   REF 0106   DATA SET ID-'7283'
    NAME-SCSFL LOBBYING GROUP 3RD   MD=GE 20
    LOC   156 WIDTH 2   DK 3 COL 17-18

              Third most successful organization.
              ....
              <For the full question text of this variable see Ref. No. 104>

              SEE NOTE(S) 1

        16   00. Veterans' <organizations>
        12   01. Professional organizations
        16   02. Educational organizations
        28   03. Agricultural organizations
         9   04. Financial organizations
        28   05. Labor organizations
        21   06. Governmental units
         5   07. Civic organizations
         5   08. Corporations

THE ILLINOIS LOBBYIST SURVEY

(CONTINUED)

```
     5      09. Religious-Charitable <organizations>  *&*
    11      10. Trade and Industrial associations    *-*

     1      20. ILLEGAL CODE  *BLANK*

    72      99. NA  *9*
```

```
VAR 0107                        REF 0107              DATA SET ID-'7283'
    NAME-FDRL GOVT END DSCRMTN       MD=GE 9
    LOC  158 WIDTH  1               DK   3 COL 19
```

C8a. Below are five statements concerning policies at various levels of government. Please indicate whether you agree or disagree with each statement.

The Federal government should take a greater role in ending all racial discrimination.
....

```
    91      1. Agree
   127      5. Disagree

    11      9. NA
```

```
VAR 0108                        REF 0108              DATA SET ID-'7283'
    NAME-GIVE S.S TO THE STATES      MD=GE 9
    LOC  159 WIDTH  1               DK   3 COL 20
```

C8b. The Federal government should turn its Social Security programs over to the States.
....

<For the full question text of this variable see Ref. No. 107>

```
    35      1. Agree
   179      5. Disagree

    15      9. NA
```

THE ILLINOIS LOBBYIST SURVEY

```
VAR 0109                        REF 0109              DATA SET ID-'7283'
    NAME-RECOGNIZE RED CHINA        MD=GE 9
    LOC  160 WIDTH  1               DK  3 COL 21
```

C8c. The U. S. should recognize Red China.

<For the full question text of this variable see Ref. No. 107>

```
     29         1.  Agree
    179         5.  Disagree

     21         9.  NA
```

```
VAR 0110                        REF 0110              DATA SET ID-'7283'
    NAME-END ALL ADC                MD=GE 9
    LOC  161 WIDTH  1               DK  3 COL 22
```

C8d. The Illinois legislature should end completely ADC and associated programs due to abuse.

<For the full question text of this variable see Ref. No. 107>

```
     40         1.  Agree
    175         5.  Disagree

     14         9.  NA
```

```
VAR 0111                        REF 0111              DATA SET ID-'7283'
    NAME-AID ONLY FOR ALLIES        MD=GE 9
    LOC  162 WIDTH  1               DK  3 COL 23
```

C8e. The U. S. should discontinue foreign aid to all countries not willing to fight for us.

<For the full question text of this variable see Ref. No. 107>

```
     94         1.  Agree
    116         5.  Disagree

     19         9.  NA
```

THE ILLINOIS LOBBYIST SURVEY

VAR 0112   REF 0112   DATA SET ID-'7283'
    NAME-LBRL-CONSERVATIVE INDEX   MD=GE 9
       LOC 163 WIDTH 1   DK 3 COL 24

R's score on the Liberal-Conservative Index.
....

         SEE NOTE(S) 2

         12   0. Conservative
         32   1. Tend to be Conservative
         49   2. Leans toward Conservative
         69   3. Leans toward Liberal
         48   4. Tends to be Liberal
         12   5. Liberal

          7   9. NA

VAR 0113   REF 0113   DATA SET ID-'7283'
    NAME-PERCEIVED ROLE AS LBYST   MD=GE 9
       LOC 164 WIDTH 1   DK 3 COL 25

C9. Briefly how would you describe your work as a legislative agent within the legislative process in Illinois.
....

         SEE NOTE(S) 3

         76   1. Contact-man
         35   2. Informant
         36   3. Watchdog
         13   4. Strategist-Lobbyist
         23   5. Contact-Informant
         18   6. Informant-Watchdog
         24   7. Mixed

          4   9. NA

APPENDIX

NOTE 1- The response categories listed for this question are of the forced-choice variety. The respondents were required to choose among the presented alternatives, except in the few cases where "Other" responses were allowed.

NOTE 2- A respondent's score on the liberal-conservative index was constructed from his responses to questions C8a, C8b, C8c, C8d, and C8e (REF. NOS. 107 to 111). However the algorithm used for computing this index is not currently available from the ICPR. Interested users must contact the principal investigators.

NOTE 3- This "role-orientation" variable is based upon a subjective decision by the investigator. The relevant data are from open-ended question C9. The ICPR has no further information for this variable.